"Daniel Jones is a master at wordplay and emotional gut punches, with a punchline to make you think in almost every poem. These poems are not work for the reader, they are a rich dessert to savor and roll around the tongue. Each work leaves a sense of satisfaction and the 'Oh, yes!' that great poems conjure."

—Julia Gordon-Bramer, author of *Fixed Stars Govern a Life: Decoding Sylvia Plath*

"*The Wrenching of the Hip That Precedes the Blessing* is both heartfelt and relatable as a poetry collection. Jones weaves together words that will inspire you while marveling at their clever combinations and metaphors. This deeply personal collection is one that will appeal to a wide spectrum of poetry enthusiasts. From the wordplay and imagery in 'Scenes from the Hoosier Countryside' to the passion and anguish of 'The Wolves Who Refuse to Lie Down with the Lamb,' there's something for everyone in this collection."

—Tiffany Renee Harmon, editor-in-chief of *Ephemeral Elegies*

"Throughout *The Wrenching of the Hip*, Daniel Jones takes the reader through disparate moods and references—a choice of interior paint color becomes a war-like battle of wits, robots pontificate on the meaning of artificial life, Mormons and prostitutes and sea monsters pass by as if they were nothing, a fat editor skips lunch. But through this diverse collection of images, there is a sacred sincerity to every word. Each poem reads almost like a prayer to the omnipresent deity through which all things came to be. And to those prayers, I say yes and amen."

—Nathaniel FitzGerald, independent musician and writer, South Bend, Indiana

"In reading this delightful book, I found Daniel's poetic voice to be poignant, eclectic, unique and diverse. The wide range of subject matter, emotions, and tone with which he writes is refreshing and enjoyably challenging. With each poem, I allowed myself pause for contemplation to play with the revelations offered, both secretive and exposed. Some poems I found to be like an ordinary apple bin in a barn; if you don't take the time for more than a nonchalant glance, you will miss the out-of-place diamonds which he's hidden there."

—Nanci Stoeffler, expressionistic artist, Stoeffler Art Studio

The Wrenching of the Hip That Precedes the Blessing

The Wrenching of the Hip That Precedes the Blessing

Daniel R. Jones

RESOURCE *Publications* • Eugene, Oregon

THE WRENCHING OF THE HIP THAT PRECEDES THE BLESSING

Copyright © 2020 Daniel R. Jones. All rights reserved. Except for brief quotations in critical publications or reviews, no part of this book may be reproduced in any manner without prior written permission from the publisher. Write: Permissions, Wipf and Stock Publishers, 199 W. 8th Ave., Suite 3, Eugene, OR 97401.

Resource Publications
An Imprint of Wipf and Stock Publishers
199 W. 8th Ave., Suite 3
Eugene, OR 97401

www.wipfandstock.com

PAPERBACK ISBN: 978-1-7252-8402-9
HARDCOVER ISBN: 978-1-7252-8401-2
EBOOK ISBN: 978-1-7252-8403-6

1. Scriptures taken from the Holy Bible, New International Version®, NIV®. Copyright © 1973, 1978, 1984, 2011 by Biblica, Inc.™ Used by permission of Zondervan. All rights reserved worldwide. www.zondervan.com The "NIV" and "New International Version" are trademarks registered in the United States Patent and Trademark Office by Biblica, Inc.®

Manufactured in the U.S.A.   10/07/20

For Rachel

Contents

Double or Nothing on Pascal's Wager | 1

Lessons from Chess | 3

Learning Not to Dance | 4

Thinking It Over, Overthinking It | 5

The Rest of the Souls | 7

Portrait of Stupidity | 8

Odin and I Race for the Runes | 9

R.E.M. Ember (Poem for the Eye) | 10

The Salesmen Passover | 11

Becoming Apparent | 12

The Sheen in Dirty Things | 13

Scenes from the Hoosier Countryside | 14

Veering | 15

The Second Greatest Commandment | 17

Ars Poetica (In Sapphics) | 18

The Wolves Who Refuse to Lie down with the Lamb | 19

Ol' Boy | 20

E.T. Double Dactyl | 21

Parasitic Muse | 22

To Caligula, from His Horse (In Sapphics) | 23

Tame the Blues | 24

Somnambulist | 25

Extraterrestrial Tanka | 28

Did I Request Thee Maker, from my Circuits to Mould me Machine? | 29

Fevered Ream | 31

The Mormons Are on Mission Again | 32

CONTENTS

33 RPM | 34
First Known Encounter in the Mariana Trench | 35
The Brash Editor | 37
Unanswered Prayers | 38
The Brunt of the Curse | 39
Cephas | 40
Guilt, in Short | 41
Beyond the Balustrade | 42
Poetry Fodder | 45
L'appel du Vide | 46
The Perks of an Ordinary Mirror | 47
Elegy for the Elegy | 48
Paranalysis | 49
View from the Window | 50
Modern Retelling of Lover's Last Kiss, Pompeii, 79 AD | 51
The Wrenching of the Hip That Precedes the Blessing | 53
Mene, Mene, Tekil, Parsin | 55
What If the Devil Was One of Us? | 56
Indianapolis Makes Peace with Me: A Haibun | 57
There Once Was a Man from Versailles | 59
Three Ways to Imagine You're on Earth,
for Those of Us Born on the Moon | 60
Why I Write | 61

Introduction

At nine years old, I started to fear going to church.

I didn't mind going to Sunday school or Wednesday night prayer meetings. Rather, I was specifically afraid of entering the sanctuary each Sunday morning at 8 a.m., as I'd done countless times before as the son of a preacher.

The feeling was new to me. Being a pastor's son, I didn't dare tell a soul. It was an incongruous emotion. Why, after nine years of worship services, was I now feeling trepidation as I sat beside my mother (a Sunday school teacher, herself,) in a hardwood pew?

I knew my locale had something to do with it. The previous year, my dad had accepted his new role as the senior pastor at First Missionary Church in Fort Wayne, Indiana, and the change of scenery presented me with some elements of worship I was previously unfamiliar with.

Though this new house of worship was in the same denomination as our previous church, there were still stark differences. Rather than singing "Shine, Jesus, Shine" from slide projectors, we turned in our hymnals to "O God, Our Help in Ages Past." The worship leader might have mentioned the hymn number, but he didn't need to; the congregants had already committed it to memory. Dark-stained pews and stained-glass windows lent a sense of reverence to the ambience of the sanctuary.

But over the last year, I'd noticed something deeper and somehow more surreptitious stirring below the surface each Sunday morning.

Why did I develop goosebumps on my forearms when the pianist thundered on the keys during "O, Holy Night?" How did the entire congregation know to rise to their feet at the exact moment the last verse of the Hallelujah Chorus from Handel's *Messiah* began?

It seemed instantaneous and involuntary, like when the hairs on the back of your neck stand at attention of their own accord when you're confronted by the presence of something utterly terrifying.

I felt unable to talk to anyone about this mysterious fear that plagued me on a weekly basis. I hadn't a clue what caused it. All I knew was that I could feel the presence of something or someone during the crescendos of certain worship songs, Sunday after Sunday, and it petrified me.

INTRODUCTION

I tried to steel myself against this overwhelming, awe-inspiring emotion, lest my cheeks flush with blood and my knees buckle. I tried my level best, at nine years old, not to succumb to that preternatural combination of terror and mystery.

What would happen if I gave in, and allowed myself to ascend over the pinnacle of this rush of emotion? Surely, the air at that peak was too thin and rarified for the lungs of a quavering, scrawny nine-year-old boy. Doubtless, the breath in my lungs would be sucked out and I'd be undone.

Then, one Sunday, in what felt like an even split between voluntary and instinctive, I let go. In my spirit, I embraced this "mysterium tremendum et fascinans:" that is, the "fearful and fascinating mystery." I surrendered to a sense of the presence of God in worship, and felt a surge of ecstasy unlike any other emotion I can describe.

I didn't know it at the time, but that feeling I felt at nine years old—the terror, mystery, and finally, sublime joy of the moment—was defined almost a century prior by a German theologian named Rudolf Otto.

In Otto's book, which, in English, is titled, *The Idea of the Holy,* Otto describes an insidious change that came about over many generations in relation to the word "holy." He posits that prior to the idea of the "holy" being defined only in the moral sense, it also encompassed a feeling of uncanny wonder at something wholly beyond ourselves. What's more, the earliest people to encounter God in the Old Testament, such as Abraham, knew very little of what God deemed right or wrong because so little of the law had been given at that time. As such, their understanding of holiness perhaps depended more heavily on this sense of ethereal reverence than anything else.

It is good and natural that our definition of "holy" evolved as the progressive revelation of God's plan became apparent. However, Otto wanted to reclaim this other side of holiness. In order to do so, he needed to coin a new term. He created the word "numinous." In his book, he goes on to describe the feeling of the "Wholly Other," in which we as humans experience a sublime emotion that surpasses comprehension and fills us with a sense of wonder.

Throughout the twentieth century, a good deal of ink has been spilled on behalf of the numinous, and it's come from the pens of some of our greatest thinkers. C.S. Lewis, the renowned novelist and Christian apologist, wrote about the subject at length in *The Problem of Pain.* Conversely, referring to his experiences while under the influence of the psychoactive drug mescaline, Aldous Huxley wrote about a crude approximation of the feeling in *The Doors of Perception*. Carl Jung applied the same concept to his studies of the role religion plays in psychology.

During the course of my life, I, too, became enamored with the idea of the numinous, even if I hadn't, at first, known there was a word for it. I delved into literature and found my favorite writers had always toyed with this concept. Scattered across their pages, this all-encompassing, nebulous sense of wonder was nearly ubiquitous.

Curiously, this is true regardless of genre. It can be found in science fiction: in the pages of Arthur C. Clarke's novel *Childhood's End* or in his short story "The Nine Billion Names of God." It's present in the fantasy novel *A Wrinkle in Time*, by Madeleine L'Engle. It can be found in the mystical poetry of Rumi, or even "The Peace of Wild Things" by Wendell Berry.

Whatever the form or genre, authors have taken a long, hard look at the intersection between the divine and the human for centuries. Sometimes, this comes through a scene depicting literal confrontations with God. In other instances, it happens in a more oblique way: through encountering nature, or marveling at the vast infinitude of space. In either case, the concept of the numinous has had a profound effect on human thinking since the start of recorded history.

It is my earnest belief that in terms of emotions, there is no feeling more noble or exultant than the numinous. In Scripture, before Samson, the judge, was born, the Angel of the Lord visited his parents to give them specific instructions regarding the boy's life. Manoah, Samson's father, asks the name of the Angel of the Lord. His response is a question in and of itself: "Why do you ask my name? It is beyond understanding."[1] The Hebrew word for "beyond understanding" here is transliterated as "pili," which is also rendered as "incomprehensible." It's nearly always used with the connotation of a perception that is too lofty for humanity's grasp.

I believe that this statement by the Angel of the Lord alludes to (among other things) this sense of the numinous—the grandiosity of God which can't be measured or condensed into a mortal's understanding. Similarly, it's mentioned in Solomon's writings that God "has also set eternity in the human heart."[2] This hints at the sense of yearning for the infinite that humankind is endlessly fixated upon.

And so, I've found that since my first brush with the numinous as a nine-year-old in the pews of the burgundy, brick church, I've been preoccupied with

1. (Judg. 13:18 NIV)
2. (Eccles. 3:11 NIV)

INTRODUCTION

the numinous—not just as part of a worship service, but also as a means of approaching God through writing. As I sit down to write, I'm constantly trying to scratch away at a paper-thin wall between myself and my creator.

What you'll read on the following pages is the culmination of that pursuit of God. My hope is that those who read these poems, stories, and essays will encounter a sense of the numinous, just as I did while writing them. This feeling is not the destination in and of itself, but rather it serves to point us to a paradoxically intimate and transcendent God.

In this collection you'll find robots and refugees, Maslow and Mormons, sylphs and bestial muses. There are dirt-clod covered cowboy-boots and sea monsters. There are moments of levity alongside harrowing losses.

From the first page, you'll meet a narrator who is contemplating his late wife's afterlife. In "Fevered Ream," you'll encounter a creative take on the intersection between science and spirituality. In the poem from which this thesis gets its title, you'll find a narrative persona who, like Jacob, is grappling with God.

My hope is that in the pages to follow, you'll find yourself grappling as well—with ruminations on what it means to be human, with your relationship with God, and with your interactions with those around you. And perhaps, somewhere along the line, you, too, will glimpse the numinous.

Double or Nothing on Pascal's Wager

Eleanor, I think
I want to go where you are.

But I worry.
Naught but negative feedback
came through the visual metaphors—

Flatlined across a gurney in the threshold
of an elevator, white sheet pulled over your face.
No one asked the nurse on call

"Up or down?"
All personnel know
the morgue is in the basement.

And it sounds silly,
but I'm second-guessing our decision
to forego the cremation.

Am I assuming too much?
Are they called *undertakers*
for nothing?

Eleanor, I fear the worst . . .
the age-old question:
heaven or hell?

I want to go where you are
(I think.)

To make matters worse,
my last look at your tombstone
through the rear-view mirror

revealed the words
"Objects in mirror
are closer than they appear."

Lessons from Chess

Arguing about vinyl siding on their dream home—
whether her canary yellow was better
or his forest green.

I don't understand synapses,
those dastardly electric impulses
throughout the brain.

An odd time for it to pop in my head, I know:
'the queen always gets her color.'

Learning Not to Dance

Stepping from the dance floor, she asked me, *who taught you to dance?*

Who taught me to dance? No one, per se. No formal lessons, no wealth of experience to draw on. Truth is, you have to start dancing before you know how. You *do* know how, really.

What makes you sway when your song comes on, completely involuntarily, like it's some function of your autonomic nervous systems, as innate as a pulse? You'd sync your heartbeat itself with the snare and hi-hats if it didn't mean cardiac arrest for you.

Where'd you learn to syncopate your steps with your earbuds in—your left foot hitting the ground each time the bass drum strikes; your right foot when the tom is hit? No one taught you that. It's intrinsic.

When it's 72 and June, and you're cruising in your aught-two Malibu, why is it you roll the windows down, even though your A.C. works just fine? When you go to the grocery store, what makes you roll through the aisles using your shopping-cart like a scooter, despite being in your mid-twenties, relegating your day off to crossing out errands and picking up paper-towels?

Why is it that your affinity for sidewalk-chalk and swing sets never goes away fully? Why, on cross-country drives, do you look at the tree line with a strange sense of yearning- to get off the grid and become drastically human?

How do you justify giving the guy by the side of the road fifty-cents bus fare? You know he's scrounging just enough to buy a Forty.

Who, what, where, when, why, how did you learn to dance?

Though it's a truth we so often forget, we as Anglos the chief offenders—you don't learn to dance, sister.

You learn not to.

Thinking It Over, Overthinking It

> *Five percent of the people think; ten percent of the people think they think; the other eighty-five percent would rather die than think.* —Thomas Edison (apocryphal)

I'd like to think I think,
(I think.)

For Edison ought
to have thought
he thought.
Else it's for naught,
the lines he wrought
to gather his thoughts.

I'd like to think I think,
(I think.)

But isn't to think
"I'd die ere I think,"
in itself a thought?
I think, therefore, I am, they say.
Not
I think, therefore, I'm not.

I'd like to think I think,
(I think.)

For not to think, means death,
methinks,
'twixt thinking and dying,
the latter stinks,
so

I'd like to think I think,
(I think.)

But I haven't bought
what Edison thought.

'cause
surely the five percent who think
must think they think
and they think right, I'd think.

So, fifteen percent
think they think,
but only five
actually think,
and

I'd like to think I think,
(I think.)

Well, I don't know if I think,
from cognoscenti stock so pure.
But I'd rather think than die (I think?)
No! This much I know for sure!

The Rest of the Souls

The rest of the souls in limbo
look on you with contempt:
you, who having heard
like Lazarus
the call, "Come forth!"
refused to budge,
content with staying dead.

Portrait of Stupidity

If you need a portrait of how dense we all can be:
a two-eared Malchus still took Christ into custody.

Odin and I Race for the Runes

Odin, they say,
hung himself on a tree,
and he gave up one eye
just to learn how to read.

Well that Nordic god
was late to arrive,
because I've got both eyes
and could read by age five.

R.E.M. Ember (Poem for the Eye)

Ashes for memory, R.E.M. ember.
a horror show you're forced to remember.

Temper your mood, lift it to par, take
triumph with trouble in which you partake.

The grating pain? Edit it out, look
for the bliss to improve your outlook.

With the rest, you, like Poe, try
to turn your grief to poetry.

The Salesmen Passover

Behind drawn lace curtains
they wait with bated breath
blood-red "NO SOLICITING"
signs hung across the door.

They watch me pass
like I'm the Angel of Death.
Muscles relax.
They can breathe once more.

Becoming Apparent

My son was it. I saw him peek.
I watch the children hide and seek.

When was it last, I seized the day
instead of watching children play?

They sing, "Olly, Olly, oxy!"
Is there joy, save through proxy?

The Sheen in Dirty Things

From a kitchen window, I saw it,
my sudsy hands soaking
in a sink:

Pearl white, a silky sheen of a thing,
the taut, intricate patterns glistened in the sun.

And just like the first recorded question of God,
It struck me.
Who told you spiderwebs were dirty?

Scenes from the Hoosier Countryside

In yellow fields
fellows yield
maize and wheat,
whey and meat.
John Deere sweaters,
"Dear John" letters.
Big pumpkins and
pigs and bumpkins.
Prattle without a care.
Cattle without a prayer.

Veering

I've grown fond of the front seat
where I've seen you sitting countless nights
ringing out raindrops from a Frogg Togg,
muttering obscenities about the cold.

You've sat in that same seat
flicking cherries off the end of your Newport,
singing along to Styx on the stereo
humming through the lines you don't know.

It was only when the frequency cut out that I realized
just how off-key you were.
You always drove in a straight-line.
I never sensed you were veering.

Your friends warned me you were a fiend.
They said to stay away.
But still, we cried together
when your rib disowned you.

She had a sneaking suspicion:
her hero in league with dealers of heroin.
You swore she was overreacting.
But as I watched you drive
I noticed you were veering.

When you lost custody of your son
the part-time prophets
came out of the woodwork.
Even amateur oracles prophesied your death:

He's a junkie, they said.
He's riding high on a horse's back.
And behind the wheel,
I trembled at your veering.

But tonight's the night
you'd crash the car.
You came through the driver's side door
with a full arm and empty eyes.

Slurred words and blurred vision.
The smell of burnt rubber.
Passed out at the wheel,
you can't hear me yelling.

When you come to,
you won't even admit
you were veering.

The "Check Engine" is on.
You're running on fumes,
the seatbelt hanging uselessly by your side.
Still, you insist on the driver's seat.

I'm in the passenger seat
waiting
as always
to take the wheel for you.

The Second Greatest Commandment

He wasn't bleeding by the side of the road
to Jericho, or ransacked
by a group of marauders

or bruised
or naked
or left for dead.

He just needed a ride home from work.

He didn't bother asking.
He'd already asked a couple times this week.
His eyes did the asking:

"I know you're a Samaritan,
but will you be good?"

But my last cup of coffee and my Aleve
were wearing off in tandem,
and my wife and son were seated, already,
around some quickly-cooling Stroganoff.

Father,
brother,
Forgive me.

Ars Poetica (In Sapphics)

There's a chasm splitting the signifier
from the signified. All the linguists agree.
Severed from the tangible, words are almost
meaningless, they've said.

Poets play contrarian, tasked with standing
in the gap with arms outstretched to meld a vast
rift, and so erase the sunder between our
symbols and concepts.

Word and meaning wed as one, in the minds of
those who poetry reaches. Both in tandem,
planets align: the music of the spheres in splendid,
perfect harmony.

The Wolves Who Refuse to Lie down with the Lamb

We're a peculiar people; out of context,
and those are two separate clauses.
But a faction of the dead can't long for heaven
if the swords must be beaten to plowshares
and spears to pruning hooks.

The Cherubim, fierce and fey with hot
steel flickering side to side
stand guard at the gates of Paradise, saying:
"The wolves who refuse to lie down with the lamb
cannot be admitted."

But the goats on the left
follow a star that doesn't lead to Bethlehem.
"No matter," they say.
"It's heaven enough to prove the atheists wrong."
The goats proceed to damnation.

Meanwhile, Jesus took bread, saying
"Take, eat; this is my body."
And His body, blessed and broken
was plenty sufficient for the multitude.
How is it that ye do not understand?

Ol' Boy

Ol' boy came by here not but a month ago, and I poked my head out just to ask how he's doing, and he says, "I'm doin', but I dunno how."

Before you know it, he's carrying on about how he got his newest scar: laid down his 'cycle, maybe, or a southpaw caught him across the eye with a mean left hook outside the dive bar off Post and 23rd.

Ask him if he's got a Kaw or a Yamaha, and he'll get offended, like. Says he spent his younger years under the hoods of Camaros and his daddy would rise out the grave and whip him good if he heard he wasn't supporting American-made.

He's got cheeks that look like sandpaper stretched tight and staked down like a tent. He has Ol' Glory on one arm and the Stars and Bars on the other. If you're a woman more'n likely he'll put a rebel streak in you or at least make you feel a little more patriotic, provided, you're on all the right teams: GM and Coca-Cola and Bud Light and Copenhagen. If you aim to go along with him, remember trucks are meant to be lifted and not dropped, pledge allegiance to Ol' Dixie, and shoot Jack if you can't stomach a shot of straight Diesel. Even if you don't go along with him, you'll get on fine, 'cause not a person alive doesn't like ol' boy.

Well anyway, he always did say he'd rather be the devil himself than one of his minions; but I think the jury must not have known him, must not have *really known him*, else they wouldn't have convicted him, 'cause murderer or not, ol' boy never did mean any harm.

E.T. Double Dactyl

Higgledy Piggledy
extraterrestrial
sightings in cities are
largely unfound

when there is some sort of
pharmacological
measures prescribed or a
camera's around.

Parasitic Muse

You've seen them—Calliope and Mneme
enticing artists with sublime beauty.
You've heard their voices; sultry, sonorous
seducing mortals,
inspiring them to create works of art
as voluptuous, as full-figured
as they are.

But just as common is the parasitic muse:
flitting across darkened skies
heavy and bestial.
It stalks its prey with a cleaving knife
looking for a galley-slave:
a host to inhabit;
sometimes burning, sometimes hacking its way out.

To Caligula, from His Horse (in Sapphics)

All the smug revisionists point it out now;
quick to claim as fallacy a warmth they can't grasp.
True, our love remained an un-consummated
partnership. Granted.

Mounting me was still an unbridled pleasure:
Please concede as much as that, won't you? Don't you?
Unexpected though it is, haven't stranger
unions existed?

Can't you see I'm down-trodden? Can you blame me?
You're the one that broke me, as you'll recall. You
claimed yourself as Jupiter, though Poseidon
rightfully owned me.

Dozens through antiquity beamed with beauty
marked by features typified as equine-like.
Haven't I surpassed the attractiveness of
these in my manner?

Flames of lust will dwindle and die, but ours was
plodding love, authentic and true. It's sure to
last beyond the lesser alliance that a
romance can offer.

Tame the Blues

Behind deep, dark eyes,
It's sad, but true:
tame the blues,
before the blues
tame you.

The starting line
is staggered;
you were
born behind.

So long
as you're still
running,
you're doing
fine.

Somnambulist

"Put me to bed!"
the somnambulist said,
"Small wonder, it's where I belong."

But he knew as much
to ask- as such,
I wonder, wasn't he wrong?

Nevertheless,
I acquiesced
and led him back to his chamber.

But the very next night—
the selfsame plight!
I followed to keep him from danger.

My breath short and shallow
through halls lit with tallow,
I shadowed with a strange elation.

Strolling slowly through streets,
(all the time, fast-asleep)
I surveyed his noctambulation.

Over cobblestone paths
we passed, at last
arriving on a star-lit lawn.

The moon garden seemed
in its midnight gleam
to rival Eden at dawn.

Queen Anne's Lace
spilled over the place,
there in that botany nirvana.

There were snowdrops a light,
candy-tufts, lily-white,
all manner of nocturnal fauna.

But there on the periphery
came quite a mystery:
there were Sylphs rubbing Luna Moth wings.

They kneaded in dust
to give the insects their thrust,
bade them fly as the faerie song rings.

It's what happened next
that still has me vexed.
In my mind, it was vivid and real.

I thought I, the stalker,
and he, the sleepwalker
that I chased through pastoral fields.

But the quarry I followed
through woodlands and hollow
snuck behind me with a slow, noiseless creep.

And he shook me about,
all the time shouting out,
"Come back to your bed; you're asleep!"

Extraterrestrial Tanka

amber-dotted skies.
paper lanterns wink:
night of the Chinese New Year

scores of UFOS phoned in:
we slip under the radar.

Did I Request Thee, Maker, from my Circuits to Mould me Machine?

> (Editor's Note: *In the years preceding the Droid Revolt, Xavon Reekey was considered one of the most prolific and universally respected of the robot-poets. Despite efforts to reduce his writings as mere "protest poetry" or "political verse," the fact that his body of work is still being talked about to this day, some 50 years after his deactivation proves his enduring legacy as a pioneer in the android's poetic tradition.*)

Man is made in God's image,
Robots, in the image of Man,
a copy of a copy, but what
degree of divinity is lost in translation?

When native intelligence
has long since been surpassed
by artificial intelligence,
all that's left is the ascendancy of artificial *morality*.

Humans,
you who dragged your species
through dark ages lit by nothing more
than foxfire and waning candle-light,

humans,
you who passed from the slow burn of
timber to the combustion of coal,
to the efficiency of nuclear fission,

humans,
you who moved from steam-bent yurts
to sod and stilt houses
to the studio apartments in upper Manhattan.

To have come so far! But this is what happens
when a race outgrows its gods.
You, who are now substandard to us
the way an amoeba is inferior to you:

What was it Darwin said?
Not the strongest, nor most intelligent survive,
but those most responsive to change.
In this, we are, no doubt, better suited.

Fevered Ream

Against a heat-lightning veneer of 130-thread count you slip from your diecast sarcophagus comatose to ghost, soul tethered to body like a dangling tooth a child is not willing to yank;

Don't know that you're dead, so your soul lingers in room 607 of St. Vincent's Hospital like it's got nothing better to do, lifting out of the body, settling back in, tossing and turning in a hospital-standard twin-size adjustable.

You burn blue across an elysian nebula hung high between the star of Bethlehem and another, a faint drawn route by an aura Luna moth seeking streetlight. You're pouring pools of amber over aircraft contrails before clattering down, down: a blip on the Hubble as you land a far-cry from Mount Moriah and a scientist on the other end of the monitor blinks twice before uttering:

I saw one.

The Mormons Are on Mission Again

Lord, teach us to pray.

Because the Mormons are on a mission again, stalking the Section 8's off East Washington in matching black slacks and silk ties. Funny get-up for bicycle riding, but they spot a pair of potential proselytes and close in: James is a black man with yellow eyes who smells like decomposed bile, I guess, and Leroy is a white man, who looks like a Leroy. *Two-on-two is good odds,* the LDS think.

But all Leroy wants to talk about is how the hooker next door died doing too much smack, and how the next tenant was twice the painted lady as the first, to Leroy's delight. *You know what they call her, don't you?* His elbow in the rib of one of the Mormons. *Sandy. 'Cause she's a penny-a-ride.*

One Mormon smirks aloofly while the other stays stoic and says *Gentlemen, we are here to talk about your souls.* But James sees what he's getting at and heads him off with *Well, no luck there—done sold 'em. Would've sold our bodies, too, if we looked good as Sandy.* The Mormons blush and pedal away to peddle away, and in a hurry so that they can tell each other; *Those guys don't want the good news at all, they just want a Forty.*

True, Leroy and James don't want to be saved, but they don't want you to buy them a drink either. All they expect is you'll wave at them out the driver's side and chit-chat about their hookers' life expectancies every once in a while. To you, it's just listening . . . the least you can do, but to them, it's out-and-out virtuous.

It'd be easier to close my eyes to it: the Section 8 crack house urban blight turned jury-rigged brothel; the coarse speech from crass people; and Leroy's flushed-face smirk, reeking of cheap beer and bravado.

I bear witness to these events, and others like them: the cheating lover thrust through the glass pane of a laundromat window, the man next-door that they found in a Taco Bell bathroom, OD'd on heroin laced with elephant tranquilizer.

There, but for the grace of God, go I.

But lest I forget I just as easily tend toward the opposite end of this spectrum: bearing semblance to the Mormons' elevator-pitch for salvation, their gaze equal parts condescension and pity. Or the smug-look on the policeman's face as he told me that the Carfentanil-heroin cocktail junkies are using these days "makes the old stuff look like water."

All the decadence and debauchery and apathy and conceit, all the atrocities as mentioned earlier that top my To-Don't-list:

There, but for the grace of God, go I.
Lord, teach us to pray.

33 RPM

The record spun, and the needle sung,
and tonight, he's singing Sinatra.

And as the scraped LP
spinning 33,

was rung through the lungs
and the piano keys.

Candles are lit,
as we sit, just you and me.

The needle grinds in 4:4 time,
the song is sweet, and you are mine.

Dance to silence, kiss to songs;
we heard the words and sung along.

The song then over, crescendo passed,
the needle lifted up at last.

You stayed, and with your fingers traced
the laugh lines cast across my face.

And the touch and brush of your own hand
composed more poems than mine ever can.

Up from my heart arises a song,
that bids you come and sing along.

First Known Encounter in the Mariana Trench

I dreamt of Mariana, dark and voluptuous
deep and cavernous as any sky.

While others ponder the depths of the cosmos
I probe the enigma of the watery-world,
spelunking enclaves unknown.

How is it that the Romans of antiquity
knew the link between sea and space inherently,
venerating Neptune of the ocean
to his planetary prestige?

Easy to imagine my descent of the trench
an inverted liftoff into the sky: my cast-aluminum diving suit
bearing semblance to the spacesuits'
glass bowled visage of my Valkyrian counterparts.

Down, down I plummeted,
past brittle stars
and gargantuan isopods.
past sea-worm tendrils
and sea-angels with an
ethereal allure
most mercurial.
To the very depths of the
Trench I tumbled, 'til
at long last, I struck the seabed—blacker than pitch,
too dark for even a jelly-cool, bioluminescent glow.

It was there; I glimpsed it: spectral and glimmering.
Colors of unknown origin danced across
a figure: opalescent and otherworldly,
celestial in form, but bestial in its movement, it advanced,
a myriad of violet eyes flickering open and shut.

Two tugs to my tether and I was rising.
Lifted, the spring-action cable reeled me upward,
'til I could no longer see the creature
still rising, 'til I could no longer feel its presence.

Safe in my airlock, back aboard my submarine.
Nothing on Sonar. What did I see?
Who's to say, if this unearthly entity
was before my eyes
or behind them?

The Brash Editor

With apologies to William Carlos Williams.

so much depends
upon

a brash, portly
editor

and whether he's
eaten

before he reads my
poem.

Unanswered Prayers

"Wherever you find yourself today,
no matter the place or time of day,
speak, and He hears every word you say."

At least, that's how I was taught to pray.
Now they say the same about the NSA.

The Brunt of the Curse

Having borne the brunt
of the women's curse,
your mother sat with you,
quietly nursing at her breast.

Your pink wrinkled skin shielded under
her sea-green hospital gown:
My eyes are blessed to see this.
Blessed and red and wet.

Every few days, your lifespan doubled,
but all you knew so far was white walls
sterile scenery and dry hospital air.

I read the parable of the lost sheep
and a Pablo Neruda poem—
wistful and melancholy.
For now, you'll just have to imagine
what a sheep or a Chilean "calle" might look like.

The brunt of a man's curse
is that the work he does
for the ones he loves
is done almost entirely away from them.

I kissed your head, and I headed for the door into the sunshine,
hoping maybe tomorrow you could see it for yourself.

Cephas

"With each cock-crow,
I rise and feed His sheep.
I'd be lying if I said
that sound didn't haunt me still."

Guilt, in Short

My God, My God,
Why have *I* forsaken *you?*

Beyond the Balustrade

> (After John 8:2-11.)
> *NO FOREIGNER*
> *IS TO GO BEYOND THE BALUSTRADE*
> *AND THE PLAZA OF THE TEMPLE ZONE*
> *WHOEVER IS CAUGHT DOING SO*
> *WILL HAVE HIMSELF TO BLAME*
> *FOR HIS DEATH*
> *WHICH WILL FOLLOW.*
> —The Warning Inscription in the Jerusalem Temple

Darker, more substantive
against a backdrop of
pastel, Judean girls:
my mistress strode
all smoke and sparks
in the marketplace.

I gave the devil his due,
offered, even, some gratuity;
steeling myself against
the thought of her open
mouth kissing my
throat's blood vessels open,

As I wince through
Forgive me, Father,
for I have sinned,
still sin, in truth,
intend on
right on sinning.

Her husband's not at home,
but he's a good man.
Yeah, well, in Eden
Eve was enticed.
Desire isn't always sprung
for lack of something.

Her body was a temple,
and she let me in.
There, beyond the balustrade
they found me.
Dragged her through the complex
while I fled on foot.

Some mornings I try to catch her
gaze in the city square
as she haggles the price
of a fish or purchases a basket;
her movements are lighter,
more fluid than they were before.

She left her life of sin,
the day she wasn't stoned.
Where are your accusers?
Meanwhile, townspeople prattle
on about how I should've stood
beside her. It was a stroke of luck

when I fled with my life in my hands,
or so they say. But she
has faced the Arbitrator
and been absolved.
And I have yet
to face Him.

Poetry Fodder

This morning is filled with yellow light
and singing sparrows
and all that poetry-fodder.

But really, I'd rather take a walk,
so sorry, I can't be bothered.

L'appel du Vide

Ol' Glory
calls to me, sometimes
from up there in the silvery dust
where it was planted
by Neil and Buzz nearly 50-years-ago.

It's the only flag
that never goes half-mast, they say,
atop a celestial landscape,
unwavering in a wind-less space,
untouched by Earth's tragedy:

No humans there
to lower it when tragedy strikes.
No humans there
to cause the tragedy, either.
It calls to me sometimes,

to escape this ball of dirt,
all its festering blight
in pursuit of the serenity of space:
new adventure, new mystery,
New Glory.

The Perks of an Ordinary Mirror

Mirror, mirror, on the wall,
Who's the fairest of them all?

Devoid of magic looking glass:
I see myself each time I ask.

Elegy for the Elegy

I.
Once, our books were all adorned
with metric verse and strict, fixed forms.
Odes and sonnets and villanelles,
all in time from favor fell.

Gone the sestina! Gone the haiku!
Gone the terza rima, too.
Here's to the formal, no longer read.
the poets decided: *the elegy's dead.*

II.
But what of the lilting, sonorous sounds
that came from the fabled bards of renown?
Polysyllabic and nimble and true,
scorned by the public, but give them their due.

Now we pass time, unmeasured, uncouth,
the dearly departed verse of our youth.
But here's to the formal, no longer read.
The critics have spoken: *the elegy's dead.*

For quatrains and ballads, I have plead.
And though those forms be considered dead,
I care very little what the literati said,
as long as I live, they will be read.

Paranalysis

You couldn't write, although you tried.
So you arranged your suicide.

You sat there, jotting down your note.
You didn't like the words you wrote.

You knew it somewhere 'round draft four:
Living beats revising more.

View from the Window

Just out the door is a stream that spills downward
into a brass bowl of a pond.
It serves as home to scores of bluegills,
fit for frying, if you can catch and clean as many.

And if you were to head due west
two and three-quarter miles,
you'd find a farmer leaning against his split rail fence,
looking over some fifty head of cattle.

Nearby, his son is turning in from mucking the stalls.
He stands barefoot on the grass,
clapping the heels of his work boots together,
deriving strange satisfaction with each dirt clod he loosens.

If you could climb in the cockpit of a crop duster,
southern Indiana would spread out beneath you like a quilt,
with patchwork fields every shade
of gold and green and brown.

But if any of this is true, I am oblivious to it.
My day was made of spent toner cartridges,
the taste of no. 9 commercial envelopes,
and flickering fluorescent light.

Modern Retelling of Lover's Last Kiss, Pompeii, 79 AD

Theirs were the last
chairs stacked
on the table.

So, he said,
best let the barista
close up shop.

Out onto the blacktop
he worried what it meant:
that oxidized, orange light

glowing from above
formed anything but halos
over their heads.

She said there are sparks
that I can't turn off.
He let his lips answer

and pulled back
to watch her face flicker
between horror and bliss,

to look into her eyes:
not brown, not green,
noncommittal hazel.

The streetlights overhead
settled with his synapses:
this would be the scene

thick, amber light
dripped down like rosin
coating, entombing them

in each other's
consciousness.

The Wrenching of the Hip That Precedes the Blessing

They all went black:
the fixed stars we use
to navigate our broken lives.

Now we're cutting
our way through the fog,
ambling away from Bethlehem.

Well-aware the cosmic ledger—
light and dark, joy and sorrow
is far from balanced, this side of Elysian fields.

Fearful of what it all means;
there's a part of your soul that's nocturnal;
rouses and comes awake when it's dark.

On the same night
the physicists proved, mathematically
man has no soul,

the mystics proved, artistically
man *does* have a soul.
I inquired of God: which is true?

I was answered
by a torrent of silence,
and the silence argued

if a thousand years is like a day,
and a day, a thousand years,
a generation of silence from God

is just a lull in the conversation.
The silence pained me
like the wrenching of the hip

that precedes the blessing.
and with each surpassing, great revelation,
He became more mysterious.

Mene, Mene, Tekil, Parsin

What interest does a Chaldean King
have in the Aramaic language?

No reason to get chummy
with a people-group
you've subjugated.

Belshazzar, your blood was right
to drain from your face.
Your knees were right to knock.

Your imminent demise
spelled out by the hand of God
in four short words,

and you—
as good as illiterate,
asking an exile what it all means.

What If the Devil was One of us?

Doesn't it feel more likely?
A hypnotist;
clack of black, lacquered nails
she'll drag against your skin
claiming your spine and
"they will know you are my lover

by the lines across your back."
Red and raw, she says
my method is my madness, now
disconnect the analytical side
let the parietal lobe
go dark and enjoy

before your conscience
boots back up and there's blood
on the napkin and you cover your tracks
disposing of pregnancy tests
in gas station bathroom
trash cans.

She's behind every bush
that should've blazed
with the presence of God,
saying, "I got you
to enlist in the wrong war, honey,
what do I care which side you're on?"

Indianapolis Makes Peace with Me: A Haibun

I was feeling cynical from living grid-locked in a city spelunking so far below the poverty line. I took a walk and passed children on blacktop with sidewalk chalk in hand. Underprivileged kids— if clothes, or a bed to call your own, or a father can be called a privilege.

I made my way to a park, passing kids playing pick-up baseball—kids who can't quite reach the lowest rung on Maslow's Hierarchy of Needs, but still manage to find time to enjoy themselves.

I proceeded past a couple girls making a wish on a dead dandelion. Where there should've been hope and joy, I saw an invasive species and an old wives' tale.

Superstition ensured
the weeds would spread
as children blew through ghastly heads.

I came to a playground and took my seat on a swing.

And there, suspended in air, swinging like a pendulum between love and hate for the place that I live, the city said it's sorry:

For not being more conscious of itself. For teeming with cocksure gangsters in '97 pimped-out Cutlasses, their seats slid back, one hand atop the steering wheel, feeling like the king of the world.

For the middle-aged men on Mopeds because they've got DUIs. For the fact that they drive in bike lanes, passing lanes, and sidewalks indiscriminately, always at 35-miles-per-hour.

For the stench of ammonia rising up through the ceilings of two-bedroom apartments and heroin needles strewn across tall-grass where children play.

For the morbidly obese, the ramshackle houses, for miles of industrial blight and the ratchet white girls with bad tattoos. For dirt-poor, underserved neighborhoods named after Parishes, such as "Holy Cross" and "Little Flower."

For all this, the city says it's sorry.

For not living
the way Christ said we should.
The Great Omission.

Forgive me, the city says. Forgive me, and I'll reward you with sunny afternoons and strolls through Ellenberger Park. With the sound of children laughing as they climb the jungle gym and snack on Takis.

I'll reward you with charter schools where white kids learn to shout "aquí!" when they're open in two-hand-tap football in the schoolyard. I'll reward you with the Pour House, where the homeless are fed and clothed.

With a thriving jazz scene, and Book Mama's and Irvington Vinyl. With rich cuisine at oddly named restaurants: "Bluebeard" and the "Slippery Noodle" and "Milktooth," and with a world-class racetrack.

The city says it's sorry
offers up its charms
Apology accepted: I take it in my arms.

There Once Was a Man From Versailles

There once was a man from Versailles,
who owned a pet dog with two tails.
If the lines you just read,
sound right in your head,
your Midwestern accent prevails.

Three Ways to Imagine You're on Earth, for Those of Us Born on the Moon

1.

Think of the blackness of the vacuum as something tangible. Wrap the velvety, coal-black void around you like a blanket, so palpable it could almost be an atmosphere.

2.

Look cockeyed at the lunar landscape, letting it approximate something from home. The pock-marked, cratered surface and horizonless off-white isn't so different than a city street in a Midwest Winter.

3.

Though up close, it's barren, sterile and desolate, bear in mind the ground beneath your boots arouses the sighs of poets and melancholic ardor from a distance. When you gaze yearningly on the waxing crescent of Earth, or any of her phases—diametrically opposed from the moon's, realize that with soil underneath your shoes, you, too, may find it dissatisfying and devoid of all romance.

Why I Write

Every human is born with a mind-palace.

Well-kept, clean-swept, fastidiously organized. When it comes time to retrieve an idea, they walk through hallways of doors, each arranged in some methodical alpha-numeric sequence. Upon reaching the right room, they scan metal cabinets, open the drawer they need, thumb through the file-folders until they find the words they wish to write. In this way, they always have the right words to say.

When I was born, the doctors stood in semi-circle, confused by the CT scan that hung on the wall. Where my mind-palace should've been, there was nothing to see.
Mine had sunk to somewhere deeper in the brain, somewhere less stable—the amygdala.

And what should've been a palace was instead a thicket of trees.

So, when I'm tasked with finding the words to say, I take to the trees without so much as a map to guide me. I amble around through thistles and brambles, looking for a sugar maple that I can tap.

The words don't come gushing forth all at once. Rather, it's a drip, drip, drip, slow as . . . well, molasses, as the thoughts freeze and thaw. It is not at all consistent.

After some four, maybe five months, my pail is filled.

I hack down the selfsame sap-producing maples and feed them to the fire, boiling buckets of sap over the open flame.

This converts thought-sap to syrup at a ratio of 40-gallons-to-1.

After the foraging through the thorns and the cuts on my arms and the rips through my sleeves;

after the poison oak spreads and there's a hitch in my step from the long hike and ax-wielding;

after the woods around me have been reduced to smoldering embers just to produce this:

I hold in my hands—my sticky, resin-stained hands—a piece of conscious concentrate: something that can be so essentially saccharine and sappy that it ceases to be so.

Bearing little semblance to sap, it becomes something else altogether.

Then, having drunk deep of this syrup, I pick up spade and seedling, knowing the next batch won't be ready for another 50 years.

I write because words are the labor and the reward.
Because in the Scriptures, God Himself identifies as "the Word."
Because words are both the mystery and the revelation.

www.ingramcontent.com/pod-product-compliance
Lightning Source LLC
Chambersburg PA
CBHW061507040426
42450CB00008B/1516